COUNTRIES OF THE WORLD

Jamaica

by Jennifer Joline Anderson

BLASTOFF! READERS, AN IMPRINT OF BELLWETHER MEDIA BY FLUTTERBEE

Blastoff! Readers are carefully developed by literacy experts to build reading stamina and move students toward fluency by combining standards-based content with developmentally appropriate text.

LEVELS

Level 1 provides the most support through repetition of high-frequency words, light text, predictable sentence patterns, and strong visual support.

Level 2 offers early readers a bit more challenge through varied sentences, increased text load, and text-supportive special features.

Level 3 advances early-fluent readers toward fluency through increased text load, less reliance on photos, advancing concepts, longer sentences, and more complex special features.

★ **Blastoff! Universe**

Reading Level

Blastoff! Beginners — Grade K

Blastoff! Readers — Grades 1–3

Blastoff! Discovery — Grade 4

This edition first published in 2027 by Bellwether Media, Inc.

For information regarding permission, write to Bellwether Media, Inc., Attention: Permissions Department, 3500 American Blvd W, Suite 150, Bloomington, MN 55431.

Library of Congress Cataloging-in-Publication Data is available at www.loc.gov or upon request from the publisher.

ISBN: 9798898800451 (hardcover)
ISBN: 9798898801694 (ebook)

Editor: Betsy Rathburn Designer: Laura Sowers

Printed in the United States of America, North Mankato, MN.

Table of Contents

All About Jamaica

Jamaica is an island country.
It lies in the Caribbean Sea.
Its capital is Kingston.

Jamaica is famous for beautiful beaches and **reggae music**.

Land and Animals

Jamaica has tall mountains. Rivers flow from the mountains. Many make waterfalls.

Rainforests lie in the valleys. White sandy beaches line the coast.

waterfall in rainforest

Blue Mountain Peak

Size: 7,402 feet (2,256 meters) tall
Famous For: the highest point in Jamaica

Jamaica is **tropical**. The weather is hot all year. October and May are very rainy.

Hurricanes form over the ocean. They can cause **damage** on land.

Hummingbirds and giant butterflies live in mountain forests. Manatees swim along the coast.

red-billed streamertail hummingbird

Animals of Jamaica

red-billed streamertail hummingbird

Homerus swallowtail butterfly

West Indian manatee

Jamaican iguana

Iguanas look for fruit and leaves to eat.

Life in Jamaica

Most Jamaicans live in cities. Nine out of ten Jamaicans have an African **background**.

People speak English and **Jamaican patois**. The most common religion is **Christianity**.

English:
Hello! What's going on?

Jamaican patois:
Ello! Wah gwaan?
(EL-oh! WAHG-wan?)

Jamaicans enjoy sports.
They play soccer and **cricket**.
They go swimming at the beach.

Reggae music is a special part of Jamaican **culture**.

Salted fish with ackee fruit is a favorite Jamaican meal. Jerk chicken is spicy!

Jamaican Foods

salted fish with ackee fruit

jerk chicken

bammy

toto

Bammy is flatbread. *Toto* is a sweet coconut cake.

In July, people gather for Reggae Sumfest. It is a music **festival**.

Independence Day is August 6. People wear black, green, and gold. These are the colors of the Jamaican flag!

Reggae Sumfest

Independence Day

Jamaica Facts

Size:
4,244 square miles
(10,991 square kilometers)

Population:
2,823,713 (2024)

National Holiday:
Independence Day (August 6)

Main Languages:
English and Jamaican patois

Capital City:
Kingston

Famous Face

Name: Bob Marley

Famous For: making reggae music popular around the world

Religions

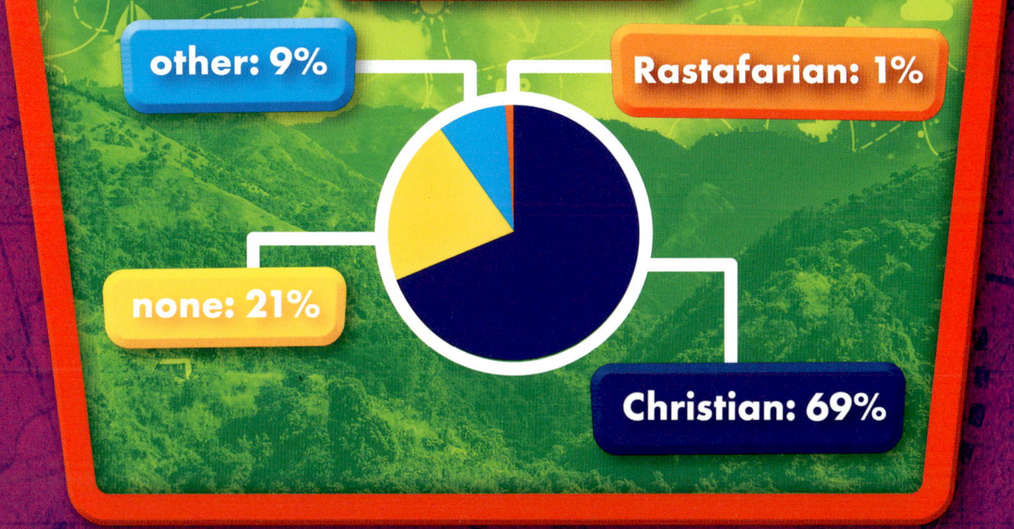

Top Landmarks

Bob Marley Museum

Dunn's River Falls

Montego Bay

Glossary

background—a person's experiences, knowledge, and family history

Christianity—a religion based on the teachings of Jesus Christ and the Christian Bible

cricket—a field game that is similar to baseball

culture—the beliefs, arts, and ways of life in a place or society

damage—hurt or harm

festival—a time or event of celebration

hurricanes—powerful storms that begin over the ocean and can move onto land

independence—related to freedom from being under control of someone or something

Jamaican patois—a language that mixes English with African languages

rainforests—thick, green forests that receive a lot of rain

reggae music—a style of music from Jamaica known for its strong beat

tropical—having to do with a place that is hot and wet

To Learn More

AT THE LIBRARY

Mather, Charis. *A Visit to Jamaica*. Minneapolis, Minn.: Bearport Publishing, 2023.

Peterson, Megan Cooley. *How Does a Hurricane Form?* Minneapolis, Minn.: Jump!, 2024.

Sánchez Vegara, Maria Isabel. *Bob Marley*. London, U.K.: Frances Lincoln Children's Books, 2025.

ON THE WEB

FACTSURFER

Factsurfer.com gives you a safe, fun way to find more information.

1. Go to www.factsurfer.com.
2. Enter "Jamaica" into the search box and click 🔍.
3. Select your book cover to see a list of related content.

Index

The images in this book are reproduced through the courtesy of: AlexDreamliner, front cover; Aide, front cover; Cetin, p. 3; Maritime Art Blog, pp. 4-5; Andreas, p. 6; PhotoSpirit, pp. 6-7; lucky-photo, pp. 8-9; Arnett Murry, p. 9; Andrew, pp. 10-11; Bernie Duhamel, p. 11 (red-billed streamertail hummingbird); ChicagoPhotographer, p. 11 (Jamaican iguana); Phil Lowe, p. 11 (West Indian manatee); DEA / V. GIANNELLA/ Getty Images, p. 11 (Homerus swallowtail butterfly); Debbie Ann Powell, p. 12; Danita Delimont, pp. 12-13; Randy Brooks - CPL T20/ Handout/ Getty Images, p. 14 (cricket); vale_t/ Getty Images, pp. 14-15; Lost Mountain Studio, p. 15; cdkproductions, p. 16 (salted fish with ackee fruit); rav0206, p. 16 (jerk chicken); Jongleur100/ Wikipedia, p. 16 (*bammy*); miss, p. 16 (*toto*); Jeremy Edwards, p. 17; Shelby Soblick/ Getty Images, p. 18; AFP/ Stringer/ Getty Images, pp. 18-19; somartin, p. 20 (flag); Dennis Morris, p. 20 (Bob Marley); Jon Arnold Images Ltd/ Alamy, p. 21 (Bob Marley Museum); Greg Meland, p. 21 (Dunn's River Falls); Aide, p. 21 (Montego Bay).